MID TO LATER ELEMENTARY

KEYBOP VOLUME 1

BY JASON SIFFORD

ISBN 978-1-70514-175-5

EXCLUSIVELY DISTRIBUTED BY

Visit Hal Leonard Online at
www.halleonard.com

Contact us:
Hal Leonard
7777 West Bluemound Road
Milwaukee, WI 53213
Email: info@halleonard.com

In Europe, contact:
Hal Leonard Europe Limited
42 Wigmore Street
Marylebone, London, W1U 2RN
Email: info@halleonardeurope.com

In Australia, contact:
Hal Leonard Australia Pty. Ltd.
4 Lentara Court
Cheltenham, Victoria, 3192 Australia
Email: info@halleonard.com.au

FROM THE COMPOSER

Welcome to **KEYBOP**! The music here is inspired by a variety of jazz and popular styles from ragtime to blues, rock, and modern.

As you learn these pieces, keep in mind that the printed music is only a starting point. Your ear and your personality play important roles in interpreting the music as well, so if you feel like changing a dynamic marking, an articulation, or even some rhythms and notes here and there, please feel free to do so! The important thing is the *groove*, so keep that beat steady and fill the room with great music!

About the Optional Accompaniments

All of the music is suitable for solo performance at recitals and festivals, but I also hope you'll take advantage of the optional accompaniments. They're written in such a way that they support the melodies and rhythms of the solo parts, giving students an extra bit of help with some of the trickier rhythms and providing a fuller sound in performance.

Note to Teachers

In addition to being catchy tunes on their own, these pieces have been written to provide you with many opportunities to help teach fundamental musicianship to your students. For example, several tonal and rhythmic patterns appear in multiple pieces. The opening melody of "Slurry Scurry" appears again in "Speed Bump," and the two pieces also share some important LH harmonies. Both pieces also feature a neighbor-note figure (A-B-A) at an important moment in the form.

For this reason, I recommend learning several pieces in the book and encouraging students to find these little moments in the music. Ask questions like: "Where else have we seen D-E-F in our melody?" or "What other piece had a lot of half steps from A-sharp to B?" Once students start to make these kinds of connections and recognize patterns in their music, their reading ability will really take off!

One of the things you'll notice about this book is that I've made use of many eighth-note rhythms at a level where students may not have encountered them yet in their method books. If that's the case, simply teach the pieces by rote and use them to prepare the student's ear for their initial encounter with these rhythms in their methods. You may also find the pieces useful as supplementary reinforcement to the eighth-note pieces in their repertoire books. In both these cases, I find "Nightfall" and "The Wriggle Rag" to be particularly useful.

But above all, enjoy the music. And thank you for making these pages part of your musical life.

Optional Accompaniment

[Student plays one octave higher than written.]

Jason Sifford

Undercover

Jason Sifford

Optional Accompaniment

[Student plays one octave higher than written.]

Jason Sifford

Beeline

Jason Sifford

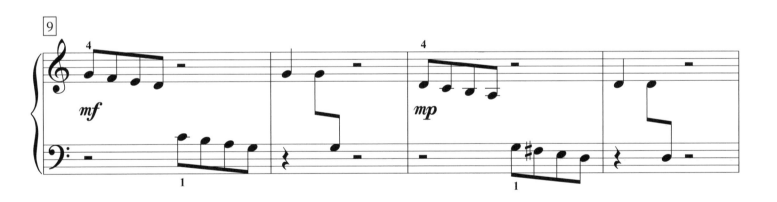

Optional Accompaniment

[Student plays one octave higher than written.]

Jason Sifford

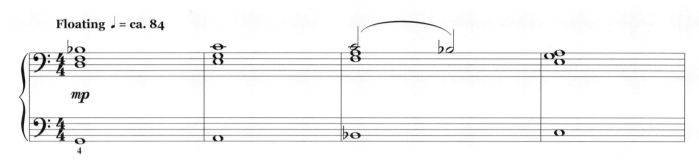

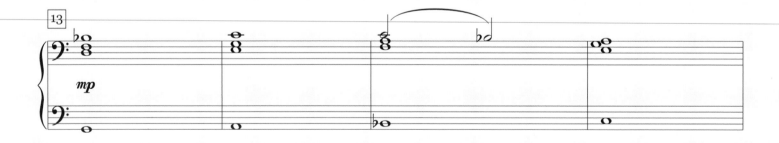

Nightfall

Jason Sifford

Optional Accompaniment

[Student plays one octave higher than written.]

Jason Sifford

Ragtime two-step ♩ = ca. 144

The Wriggle Rag

Jason Sifford

Ragtime two-step ♩ = ca. 144

Optional Accompaniment

[Student plays one octave higher than written.]

Jason Sifford

Tumble

Jason Sifford

Optional Accompaniment

[Student plays one octave higher than written.]

Jason Sifford

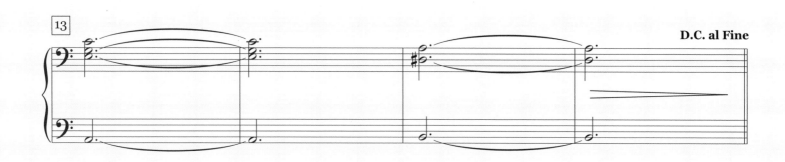

Pendulum

Jason Sifford

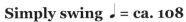

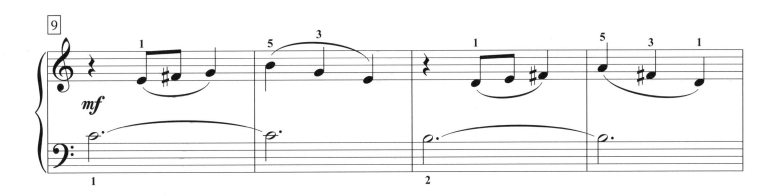

Optional Accompaniment

[Student plays one octave higher than written.]

Jason Sifford

Slurry Scurry

Jason Sifford

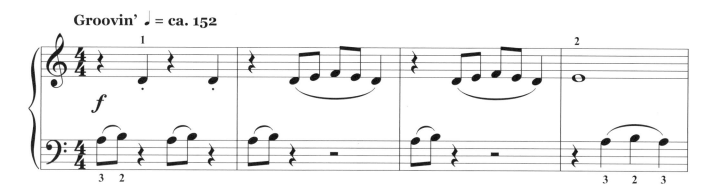

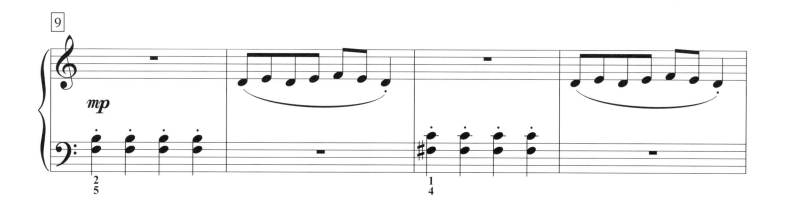

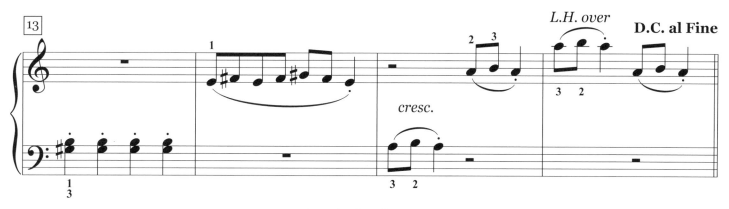

Optional Accompaniment

[Student plays one octave higher than written.]

Jason Sifford

Turbo

Jason Sifford

Optional Accompaniment

[Student plays one octave higher than written.]

Jason Sifford

Atmosphere

Jason Sifford

Optional Accompaniment

[Student plays one octave higher than written.]

Jason Sifford

Not too fast! ♩ = ca. 132

Speed Bump

Jason Sifford

Not too fast! ♩ = 132

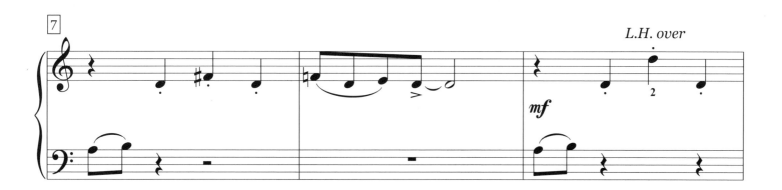

Optional Accompaniment

Gruntled

Jason Sifford

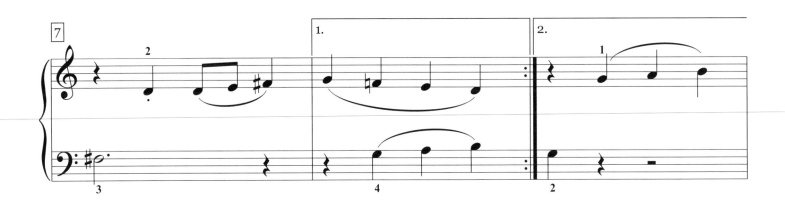

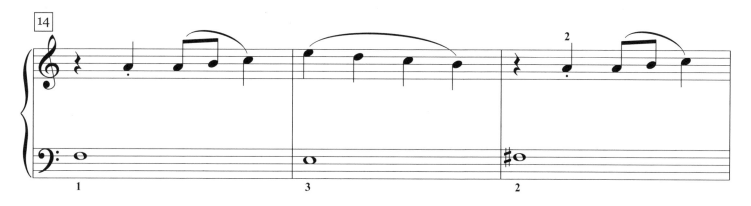

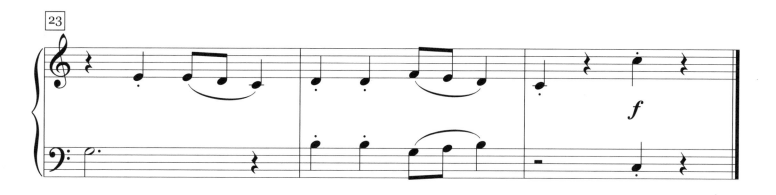

YOU ARE NOW READY FOR

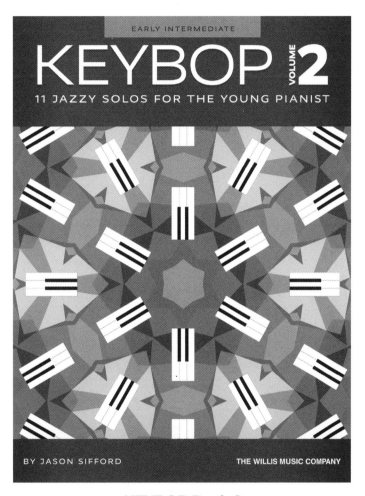

KEYBOP Book 2

Early Intermediate | HL00368669

ALSO FROM JASON SIFFORD

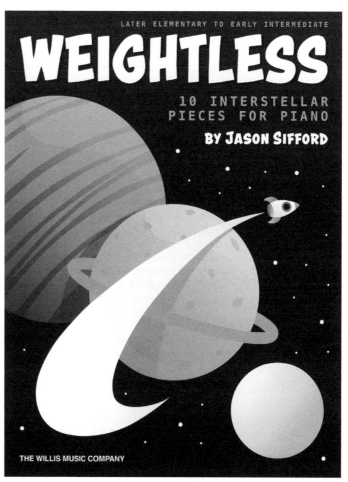

Beware the Jabberwock
8 Original Piano Pieces Inspired by Lewis Carroll
Early Intermediate
HL00290023

Weightless
10 Interstellar Pieces for Piano
Late Elementary to Early Intermediate
HL00327629